Welcome to Rockdale Co. GA.

"The Night the Lights Went Out in Georgia "(https://en.wikipedia.org/wiki/The_Night_the_ Lights_Went_Out_in_Georgia)" is a Southern Gothic song, written in 1972 by songwriter Bobby Russell and sung by Vicki Lawrence, an American singer, actress, and comedian. Vicki Lawrence's version, from her 1973 Bell Records album of the same name, was a number-one hit on the Billboard Hot 100 after its release. In addition to several other renditions, the song was again a hit in 1991 when Reba McEntire recorded it for her album For My Broken Heart. McEntire's version was a single, as well, reaching number 12 on Hot Country Songs.

The reason for this introduction is to illustrate the true nature of Georgia's ongoing status as a Police State where making false arrest, fabricating charges and falsifying documentation are just part of Georgia's normal police state activities though this seems to have become commonplace throughout the country. Also commonplace is the following; while working as an intern for the county works of Newton Co. I had spoken with an employee of Newton Co. who confirmed what has always been known or at least believed which is that the police in many states deliberately target the law abiding citizens primarily because they will most likely never have a chance in court.

The purpose for this targeting is strictly for the mass extraction of funds. Obviously, they never target welfare type recipients. In fact, it has been said and confirmed, that of the known crimes committed, only 10% are ever addressed and about 2% are successfully prosecuted. Of that 2%, it is believed that possibly half are innocent, at least according to this particular county employee.

You will notice that the majority of this brief will focus on the counties of Rockdale and

Newton. These two counties alone, are responsible for more mishandling of legal-ilegal matters than most of Georgia's counties combined as will be illustrated.

In 1979, at the Lexington Village Apartments (today known as Town Point Apartments) in the city of Conyers of Rockdale Co. Ga., two little girls, both about the ages of eight years old, were found dead. Their bodies were discovered by their mothers, hanging from a swing set.

When both the Conyers and Rockdale Police responded to the scene, they immediately had the coroner collect the bodies without ever conducting an investigation, simply put, they literally wrote off this horrific event by stating the two girls were just playing and somehow managed to hang each other. No further details were ever given.

The obvious question is, how in the hell could two little girls accomplish this and how in the hell could the police simply blow this off as a mere oops?!?!? In spite of how absurd this sounded, both police departments maintained their views and closed the book on the case completely, or more appropriately said, they just turned their backs on this terrible tragedy. No reasonable explanation would ever be given as to how this could have happened. It is impossible to imagine that two little girls were somehow able to hang each other simply by playing at the playground.

This tragic story was passed on to me in 1986 by Francis Mullins, who was the manager of the Lexington Village Apartments at the time. From this point on, I will refer to the Lexington Village Apts appropriately as Town Point Apts.

The Atlanta Child Murders, (https://en.wikipedia.org/wiki/Atlanta_murthat ders_of_1979%E2%80%9381) known locally as the "missing and murdered children case", was a series of murders committed in Atlanta, Georgia, from the summer of 1979 until the spring of 1981. Over this two-year period, at least 28 African-American children, adolescents, and adults were killed. An Atlanta African-American, Wayne Williams, 23 years old at the time of the last murder, was arrested and convicted of two of the adult murders.

With the case closed on just two adult victims, investigations into the remaining murders were immediately halted leaving them deliberately unsolved to this day. But, the story doesn't end there; in fact, it has been widely held throughout the country that the parents were actually responsible for the deaths of their own children. Proof of this 'statement' follows:

While I was attending the Non-Commissioned Officers (NCO) Academy in Macon Ga in the late 80s, the events of the missing and murdered children's case was being revisited by some of the attending soldiers who like myself were all reservist. One of the reserve members in attendance was an Atlanta S.W.A.T. member who was part of the investigation. He graciously confirmed that the parents had indeed killed their own children. However, this info was completely and deliberately averted to mislead the public.

In fact, the S.W.A.T. officer went on to say that the FBI, the GBI (Georgia Bureau of investigation) and the Atlanta Police were all well aware of the fact that the parents had killed their own children which probably means an innocent man is in prison for crimes he may not have committed, and I'm not alone in this view.

One can only speculate as to what may have triggered the parents to suddenly start killing their own children. The swat officer stated that no one in authority could give a ligament explanation as to why this cover up was needed outside of some kind of political bullshit. However, once Wayne Williams was convicted, the murders had indeed ended, or so the authorities said. The truth is, the murders never ended, in fact, children and adults are still being murdered in Atlanta and all across the country to this day.

This presents a clear picture as to why both the Rockdale Co. and the Conyers Police Depts. felt the need to covered up the true nature of the deaths of the two girls; it prevented any potential connection to the horrific cover-up of what was happening in Atlanta since both cases appeared identical and timely.

Because of the honor and integrity that exist among most military personnel, I have agreed to maintain the officer's anonymity.

Around 1985, Sheriff Vick Davis of Rockdale Co. was accused of stealing county funds, supplies, equipment and illegally using inmate labor for personal gain by building a barn and other storage facilities on his private property.

It didn't take long for this story to reached the WSB Channel 2 News of Atlanta from an anonymous tipster. While Sheriff Vick Davis was being interviewed by a WSB News reporter just outside of the Rockdale county jail concerning this matter, he became so irate that he brutally assaulted the reporter sending him to the Rockdale County Hospital's emergency room, all of which was caught on camera. The sheriff was brought up on charges, by both the news station and the individual reporter but even with more than enough evidence to convict the average person, Sheriff Vick Davis somehow managed to weasel out of these charges.

Also during this same time period, some of the Rockdale sheriff's deputies under Sheriff Davis were caught selling guns on duty and in their patrol cars at night by undercover reporters of yet again, Channel 2 News. This information too came from a tipster. These guns were being sold to a variety of customers, customers who did not even have the proper credentials (background checks).

Sheriff Davis and the attornies for Rockdale Co. stated that no rules or laws were broken since the weapons were not stolen and all gun sells were legally conducted. Really? Question is, shouldn't the patrol cars be used for patrolling the streets? Why do the police need to sell guns and why can't these "customers" buy guns from a store? No extensive investigation was ever conducted into these cases. In either case, Internal Affairs just looked the other way.

Sheriff Vick Davis simple skated again and is now serving as a North Carolina State congressman. I guess crime does pay, and by the looks of it very well, that is for the Rockdale elites.

In 1986, Jerry Farmer, a 20 veteran of the Conyers Police department at the time, made a sudden transition from the police dept. to begin working as head of maintenance for the aforementioned Town Point Apts. Mr. Farmer had only been with the Town Point Apts a couple of months before he was caught stealing refrigerators and other items from the apartment complex. It was said but unconfirmed that he had also stolen personal items from some of the residences as well. Imagine that, a recent former cop wasting no time stealing which could possibly mean he has been doing this all alone in other places under the guise of a Conyers Police Officer. Once again, the average person such as you and I would have easily been arrested and convicted.

The conclusion to the event should come as no surprise, but to save face among other things for the police, Jerry Farmer was given a deal cut by the Conyers & Rockdale County police with the City of Savannah Ga., allowing Jerry Farmer a lateral transfer to be reinstated as a police officer for the Savannah Police Dept., where he remains to this day. His wife, Sandy Farmer, also a Conyers Police officer left the dept shortly after this incident to begin working as the manager for the same Town Point Apartments. They also ceased being a couple during this time period as well.

The Conyers Motor Inn is located in the heart of Conyers, on Iris Dr. It has been well believed to conduct business dealings involving prostitution, drugs, and murder, just to name a few of it's more notable attributes. However, the motel is hardly known to have ever conducted a dime's worth of legitimately business.

So after decades of operation, with only a rare car or two to be seen in the parking lot, one might ask, how does it stay in business? Simple, the county and city gov't of Rockdale and Conyers are keeping it up, "allegedly" of course by trafficking drugs and operating a prostitution ring. It is also believed that a small flow of weapons is included on this wish list too.

In the mid-1990s, a Conyers Police Officer, Jackie Dunn, revealed to me an incident involving about 20 women that were found dead and nude behind the Conyers Motor Inn over a span of two years at this particular time. It turns out that it was all about a prostitution ring that had gone wrong under the operated of Rockdale Co. & Conyers.

Apparently, some or all of the "working girls" were going to blow the whistle on the whole racket. Originally these women were all arrested under bogus charges and were being blackmailed into prostitution raising revenue for the Rockdale elites. These women were selected specifically by the police after garnering enough info to blackmail them. The police Chief at the time was Chief Lucas while his counterpart was of course Sheriff Vick Davis. Clients include big business leaders and a variety of political figures leading all the way to the state level and possibly to the federal level.

Many on the local level included highly trusted police, lawyers, and even preachers etc. This helps to ensure loyalty and favors which allow such rackets to prosper.

Of course as already stated, this too is all alleged, even though the bodies of the many victims found behind the Conyers Motor Inn were confirmed according to Officer Jackie Dunn. These bodies were also quickly collected and buried, buried that is, in every sense of the term meaning never making the public eye. Little effort was needed to keep it out of the local paper, the Rockdale Citizen since the Rockdale Citizen is the local newspaper and is a highly controlled newspaper of the county and city government. Freedom of the press my ass!!!

Though he never suggested it, I believe that since Officer Dunn knew I was a military reservist at the time, he must have felt I might be able to expose this information more efficiently, meaning no backlash to himself. I never spoke of this until now.

Officer Jackie Dunn knew I had trained with the DEA but for just a short time while serving at Fort Stewart. I was in the infantry training in various tactical scenarios against mock-up drug cartels. During my training with the DEA, I was shown classified maps that I can confirm without a shadow of a doubt shows the DEA did indeed and may still be involved in moving weapons into central and South America and many other places around the world such as Africa. Americans have always believed this has been going on for many years, even up through the Obama Administration, (Fast and Furious). (http://www.nationalreview.com/article/430153/fast-furious-obamas-first-scandal)

Many of these weapon recipients are of some of the most nefarious organizations imaginable such as terrorist and cartels groups. The DEA has also been involved in the smuggling of drugs and people into the USA for years. Most of the people are children and young adults who are primarily earmarked for the slave sex trade. This confirms the suspicions of most Americans, also I can confirm that the CIA, HLS and especially The White House along with many other federal agencies and big business (up through Obama) were involved in this trafficking and cover-up.

To say I was amazed that the DEA actually provided maps that indicated the trade routes in red lines is the understatement of the century. These lines went through Georgia cities such as Atlanta, Athens, Rome and yes you guessed it, right through Rockdale and Newton County. The DEA stated that these open routes are for monitoring traffic.

However, under President Trump, there is no doubt that this will al come to an end. I also have credible evidence that Rockdale's lead defense attorney Elizabeth Simpson is at least partially in charge or may even be fully in charge of these matters. More on Counselor Simpson later.

In 2000, while I was stationed overseas during the Bosnian conflict, I had received a call from Rockdale Co., but this was by no means a friendly call thanking me for my services. Turns out it was from child support. At first, I thought the worst, that there might have been a terrible accident. Thank God it wasn't, instead I was being threatened by some old fat pig man-hating demon child-support lying bitch of course saying I was behind on my child support. WTF, I'm thousands of miles away in a combat zone and this psychotic bitch from child-fucking support calling me up threating to put me in jail. What has happened to rational thinking? I eventually got the mess straightened out proving I was current with my payments. Thank God I was able to move on to watch my two daughters reach that magic number, 18!!!

General Douglas MacArthur, while addressing the graduating class of West Point said to the men who were already considering marriage stated the following; "Men, before you marry I strongly suggest that you first master the art of war".

2001: It was at this time that a few veteran friends and I went to visit the Oconee National Forest after returning from our tour in Bosnia. It was pleasant until we started to leave. As we were driving toward the exit, an employee of the park, who was just ahead of us driving a park utility vehicle proceeded to make an immediate hard left turn without warning and obviously without looking which lead to an immediate collision between our vehicle and the utility vehicle.

Fortunately, no one was injured and witnesses on site validated that the employee was the one responsible for the accident. Still, the park ranger in charge went forward to interrogate us as though it was our fault. The head ranger seemed hell bent on blaming us, even checking our credentials. He even asked us what we were doing at the park, WTF!!!

The ranger never checked the employee for his credentials instead he did his best to shift the blame toward us, but it just so happened that the witnesses were rangers too. They may have been fired for telling the truth; just saying! We were finally allowed to leave and advised never to come back. Imagine that. Of course, we never returned.

The Koch Brothers (Charles G. Koch and David H. Koch), two sons of the Koch family involved in the family business and philanthropy, who are most noted for their political activities and their control of Koch Industries, which is the second-largest privately owned company in the United States with revenues reaching over $115 billion by the end of 2013. The business was started by the father, Fred C. Koch, who developed a new cracking method for the refinement of heavy crude oil into gasoline. Fred's four sons litigated against each other over their interests in the business during the 1980s and 1990s.

Today, Charles G. Koch and David H. Koch are more commonly referred to as simply, The Koch brothers – and the only two sons of Fred Koch's four sons still with Koch Industries. They have also founded and funded a number of both conservative and libertarian political organizations.

In the following article; (http://money.cnn.com/2016/01/20/news/econo my/marshall-project-koch/) Charles Koch boldly spoke of the already well-known corruption within the American legal system. In part, Charles Koch expands on how the legal system has forced innocent people to plead guilty to charges they have not committed for the sake of filling in quotas and regulating the public. The article is very informative. A must read!

On June 12th of 2006, a fellow veteran friend of mine was attacked by a black and an illegal Hispanic alien. The intent was quite obvious, to rob and inflict as much harm as possible, even to molest and murder him. However, the tides were turned as my friend beat the shit out of the two pieces of trash. He even chased them off. However the unexpected happened when the black thug, Ryan Warren actually called the police on the veteran. The illegal thug calls himself Moses. So imagine that the attackers are now the victims and were rewarded as such. Is there any reason why crime is out of control?

And yes, you guessed it, it all took place in Rockdale Co. Ga. My veteran friend was then arrested and charged with two counts of felony family violence. How in the hell can this be??? The Rockdale Police eventually lowered the charges to misdemeanor family violence. Family violence, obvious he was not related to either of these two thugs, he being white and these two thugs one being Black which says both nothing since the scum bag is nothing and a lot being a lot of trouble and the other an illegal alien which also is self-explanatory.

The actions of the Rockdale Police only proved their criminal intent which began the second they arrived on the scene; the Rockdale Police upon arrival moved with immediate and deliberate intent against the veteran telling him to write a report of what happened while the police spent approximately 30 minutes casually interview the two would be assailants.

After their apparent wonderful time of conversing and laughter with the two worthless thugs, the Rockdale police moved to charged the veteran. There was, however, one Rockdale Police officer who knew it was the two thugs who started it. He was obviously pushed into a political corner. The obvious question is how can you charge a white person with family violence when he cannot be related to either a black and an illegal latino alien. Rockdale Co. continues to prove their corruption is as vast as the universe is infinite.

Elizabeth Simpson was court ordered as the veterans defense attorney along with Sandra Goss who both acted more like prosecuting attorneys toward their veteran client, (this said because they obviously refused to do their job as his defense attorney), but instead chose to play the political corruptness game for the county of Rockdale all too well. However, at first Sandra Goss saw it differently. Sandra Goss knew this was an obvious setup and said this would be an easy win in front of a jury trial.

Elizabeth Simpson obviously went the political corruptness way using threats against the veteran to manipulate the case against him. Elizabeth Simpson also confronted Sandra Goss explaining to her to stick to the plan of betraying the vet and forcing him to take their deal they so "generously" laid out before him or else.

Understanding the system all too well, he knew to go ahead with the plan set against him meaning he was being sold out by the wolves in defense attornies clothing. While standing before the judge, he tried to explain his case, even to the point that the dates of the events were even wrong, yet the D.A. (District Attorney) some blond bimbo stated clearly that it doesn't matter what the actual dates were, just what was on her documentation.

After his case had been finalized, he was placed on probation, given a fine and was forced to go to anger management classes. While still in the courtroom, Sandra Goss was court ordered to stay with him until all proceedings were complete, this meant to sit with him and make sure he said nothing contrary to the court-ordered lies.

Both Elizabeth Simpson and Sandra Goss new that Ryan Warren had a prior arrest record for assaulting a Dekalb Co. Police Officer. He is also a homosexual and was caught having sex with his gay illegal Hispanic alien lover. Ryan Warren was also suspected of molesting his little brother of which again, Elizabeth Simpson and Sandra Goss were both well aware of. This info slipped out in court as the vet overheard as Elizabeth Simpson and Sandra Goss were seemingly in a heated discussion.

The bone-headed judge knowing there were too many inconsistencies when right along with the plan but stated how it would not go against his work record with background checks. Elizabeth Simpson argued the very thought against the judge, and against her client making it clear to the judge not to help him. Imagine an attorney arguing with the judge against her own client.

These actions of Elizabeth Simpson were nothing short of plain sabotage against her own client. Elizabeth Simpson seemed hell-bent against this veteran. Elizabeth Simpson stated that Georgia has no stand-your-ground-law which is another lie, literally stating it was illegal to defend yourself. Her explanation is you are supposed to run. What a stupid lying bitch!!!

Apparently, it seemed that the attackers had the right to attack him but he had no right to defend himself. Well, Elizabeth Simpson, this is for you sick bitches, we will defend ourselves regardless of what you and your lying ass laws say. If your laws and police can't do the job of protecting us then we will do your job for you.

Sandra Goss is no longer with the county, the cover story is she sought better opportunities, but the real story is she couldn't handle the political corruption.

The Rockdale Co. system forced the veteran to submit to their terms as a threat or they could make things worse, this from Counselor Elizabeth Simpson. As a defense attorney, Elizabeth Simpson exemplifies an attitude that is contrary to anything but what a defense attorney should be. With Elizabeth Simpson as a defense attorney, the courts have no need for a district attorney.

The vet made an attempt to contact the Internal Affairs but as you can imagine, it was useless. They actually laughed as he tried to plead his case against the Rockdale Police.

Also in 2006, in Newton Co., My daughter and grandson were involved in a traffic accident caused by an older black male who was obviously high, drunk and incoherent acting in a violent manner though did not attack anyone. The Newton Co. police seemingly took their sweet time to arrive but upon arrival had to restrain the drunk from his violent attitude.

My grandchild was only 14 months old and well strapped in his car seat and suffered no injury thanks to God, still the officer on the scene refused to call an ambulance because he knew the EMTs would force him to place the black under arrest for being obviously under the influence of alcohol which you could smell and seemingly under the influence of some type of drug.

I thought if this had been reversed, that is to say, if I (being white) had run a black off the road, what would the racial fallout have been like? The blacks would have been outraged to include riots, personal attacks, and countless rapes just for starters. The officer chose not to do his job, big surprise. No tickets were issued and no EMTs were dispatched to the scene. Way to go Newton Co.

We all managed to survive the day and move on, no thanks to the Newton Co. Police. My grandson is healthy and doing well these day thanks only to the true God of Israel.

Around 2007, a little-known incident involving a Conyers Police Officer and a motorist at the intersection of 138th and I-20 located in the northern end of Conyers. While at this intersection waiting for the light to change, I witnessed a Conyers Police Officer, a big fat bald headed cop who was behind another driver at the intersection, for no apparent reason, exited his patrol car and literally begin harassing the driver just ahead of him, From my perspective, I could see he was a young man approximately in his mid-20s.

The Conyers Police Officer just simply came up from behind the man while he too was just waiting for the light to turn green with his weapon in hand and pointing it at the driver's face only inches away. The Conyers Police officer then began yelling threats and obscenities. The driver was obviously confused and doing his best to cooperated, having his hands on the steering wheel where the officer could easily see. Yet this officer still apparently unsatisfied as he continued to yell and shake his pistol furiously in the face of the driver.

Sad to say, I wasn't able to see the conclusion of this event since the light turned green allowing traffic to proceed. A few days later I went to the local paper (the Rockdale Citizen) to see if the story had reached them but one of the editors of the paper claimed she had never heard of the incident. What a shocker.

In 2012 much like Rockdale and Conyers police, the town of Porterdale which has a population of about 1,452 residence as of 2013. It is a small piece of land about a square mile in size made up of a few roads located in Newton County. The small town has a 6-man police force of which has literally been green-lighted to harass its citizens and has done so for years. This is apparently common in many small towns in America. Here's how it all works;

The Porterdale authorities have long sent a clear message that they are above the law, having the right do anything they feel, after all, they are not actually police but HLS (Home Land Security). It's being said even now "It's time that we the people send them a clear message by taking back our freedoms, letting them know that they can no longer bully the public and that their homeland security status will not save them from the justice of the American People as outlined in the Constitution".

We the people are determined to reclaim America out of the clutches of this corrupt government for the people of America. Like most residents, I too received a ticket from the Poterdales homeland security storm trooper thugs. My ticket was for failing to go to Burger king; actually I was on my way to Burger King for a quick breakfast but after seeing how crowded it was as I was driving by, I decided to continued to exit the parking lot where one of the Porterdale HLS storm troopers came barreling through traffic complete with lights and siren nearly causing untold wrecks to desperately get to my location to serve me up with a ticket for doing what he referred to as a cut-across. What a worthless lying bastard.

There are three entrances/exits but only one has an unclear sign stating not to go across the parking lot regardless of which way you enter. This means with or without a sign to indicate you could be making a mistake means nothing except to siphon more money. As you guessed, they give neither warning nor any consideration, just tickets as they siphon money from the innocent which affects our children as well.

The Porterdale police thrive and thrill themselves as they brag about stealing money from needy families who can barely put food on their tables or buy medicines, clothing and many other basic needs let alone birthdays and Christmas etc.

The Porterdale police (HLS) have established many of these illegal traps made legal which authorizes these nazi storm troopers free unrestricted rein in their one-mile domain of terror. They give no warning, yet every ligament police department nationwide may give some consideration, sometimes. But as stated, they are not a ligament police department rather home-land-criminals.

Porterdale has been boosted literally by millions of tax dollars, all compliments of the mighty HLS to annex land such as the golf course on Brown bridge road, and out beyond hwy. 162 well in Newton Co. Porterdale also has fully outfitted combat vehicles and several new police cars yet no one to operate them, hmm. Their goal is to site every Poterdale citizen to build revenue, place everyone on a watch list and to flex their criminal muscle. Home-Land-Insecurity is pushing their storm troopers to get this done speedily.

With only about 6 officers at the time of this brief, the mighty Porterdale homeland security storm troopers write more tickets than the Atlanta police Dept. per-capita which has thousands of officers. As mentioned, all these fines come at the price of food, medicine, clothing and in some cases the loss of their homes taken from our children for the fattening of the bellies of HLS as mentioned. As I look at the fat-bellied bald headed Porterdale chief (of just six thugs), I can only wonder just how much innocent blood they can drink.

The worthless cop who thrills in writing tickets who sighted me was Kevin Courchaine, patrol car no. 308, He drives one of the hot-rod dodge vehicles. As they continue this onslaught, we watch as the country and this world is tearing itself apart. This country has become its own worst enemy by such actions as the Porterdale police and the judicial system. They abuse families and steal our children's livelihood. This is nothing short of pure legalized crimes against humanity including child abuse at its finest.

At the Porterdale courthouse, the airhead judge presiding introduced herself by making it clear with a smile how easy it is for her to send anyone to jail for a year even for a simple traffic stop, but at the end of the day, she is still just another home-land-security stooge. She also assured me I had no chance of winning, where have I heard this before? I went ahead and paid the fine. So the idiot judge ask if I'm admitting guilt, I fired back "never", I went on stating that all you want is the blood money. I then asked if any of the money would go to a charity such as children's hospitals for cancer research, she laughed with such hysterics saying never.

It goes without saying how displeased they were with my courage.

Casey Cagle is the current Lt. Governor of Georgia. I called his office to gain support with this obvious repeat of abuse by Porterdale officials. The Porterdale Police Dept. had been cited before because some of their officers had a running contest to see who could write the most tickets. When this eventually made the news, the Porterdale Police decided to act (only after it went public) by firing the officers involved in the corruption. Thought the Porterdale police admitted the corruption on the officers part, they still maintained the legitimacy of the tickets written. How the hell does that work???

So I presented my complaint to the office Lt. Governor Casey Cagle. However, in response to my request, he had his personal secretary call me back advising me of what a pathetic coward he is as she relayed to me that Casey Cagle advised me to bow-down to Porterdale, though he does acknowledge the corruption. Are you kidding me!? I advised his secretary to tell him to kiss my ass and told his secretary to tell him not to get too comfy in his political position because as a veteran, I intend to tell as many vets what a lying deceiver Cagle is. Cagle has always claimed to be such an advocate for Americans and especially for veterans, what a lying coward!

In 2016, now Sheriff Eric J Levett of the infamous Rockdale Co. made a claim that the KKK paraphernalia such as recruiting material was left on car windshields that were parked at Wal-Mart in Rockdale Co. Naturally this was a lie since none of 500+ cameras captured any images of anyone planting such material on cars and no fingerprints were found on any of the alleged paraphernalia which was supposedly packaged in plastic bags, and everyone knows that fingerprints can easily be lifted from plastics. The sheriff called this "a disturbing case" yet nothing else was ever mentioned. The so-called case vanished which was found out to have been fabricated after all. This is disturbing!!

Also in the same month, the aforementioned Sheriff Eric J Levett announced to have made a prostitution ring bust at the aforementioned Conyers Motor Inn which again, has for years been known as a sanctuary for drugs, murder, prostitution and much more, how ironic. It seemed the county of Rockdale needed to quiet the rumors about the Conyers Motor Inn. So the sheriff's dept and the city police staged a raid with claims of making several arrests, yet no name or pictures of the arrestees ever made public. Again, all this under the watchful guidance of Rockdale County's corrupt defense attorney Elizabeth Simpson and her team of legal thugs.

Just for the record, defense attorney Elizabeth Simpson currently makes upwards of $100,000 annually and an "alleged" $300,000 in kickbacks for her cooperation as well as hands-on assistance in the county corruption. I can testify that Elizabeth Simpson's corruption is definitely "Absolute Corruption".

Rockdale Co. and Newton Co. like most of this country have killed off Christianity which this country was founded on leaving a void filled by a vacuum of demonic style religions such as Islam and Satanism which are actually one in the same. The Bible said that in the end times it would be worse than Sodom and Gomorrah, looks like we're there. It's no wonder why this country and the world is in such a state of chaos and devastation.

As a result, Rockdale Co. is now experiencing a massive deficit of its county and city police officers. They have become so corrupt that they have allowed their jurisdictions to become overrun with unbelievable levels of crime. Elizabeth Simpson and the rest of the legal teams both defense and prosecution are in lockstep responsible for the collapse of Rockdale's legal system. Conyers was profiled recently by the police reality drama as one of Americas most crime-ridden cities.

They are now unable to put the genie back in the bottle therefore no longer able to maintain their positions of control within the county. Law enforcement in Rockdale Co. is out the window. It's now based on a strict system of corruption as proven by all the aforementioned dark nefarious dealings The county is even paying criminals like the local drug lords to literally contain the crime for the police.

We are now seeing across the country were the police are refusing to do their jobs or are just leaving the departments as seen in the following article, (http://nypost.com/2016/07/09/how-the-ferguson-effect-is-destroying-chicago/) The following is just a small excerpt from the article in parentheses: "Over Memorial Day weekend 2016, 69 people were shot, nearly one per hour, dwarfing the previous year's tally of 53 shootings over the same period.

The violence is spilling over from the city's gang-infested South and West sides into the downtown business district; even Lake Shore Drive has seen drive-by shootings and robberies. The growing mayhem is the result of Chicago police officers' withdrawal from proactive enforcement, making the city a dramatic example of what is called the "Ferguson effect." Not to be outdone, Rockdale Co. is picking up steam with increasing violence.

This article is by no means suggesting that all police are bad cops, but as we've seen in the past, the bad cops outweigh the good cops. The good cops are always silenced with threats leading to the cultivation of a corruption world.

There was a time in this country where the people were the law, to the point that people could defend themselves, their homes, especially their family with no consequences. In time, maybe sooner than we think, it may come back to these times in order save America. More and more True Patriotic Americans across this land are on board with this belief.